How to Change the World: The Path of Global Ascension Through Consciousness

Dan Desmarques

Published by 22 Lions Bookstore, 2019.

Copyright Page

How to Change the World: The Path of Global Ascension Through Consciousness

By Dan Desmarques

Copyright © Dan Desmarques, 2019 (1st Ed.). All Rights Reserved.

Published by 22 Lions Bookstore and Publishing House

About the Publisher

About the 22 Lions Bookstore:

www.22Lions.com

Facebook.com/22Lions

Twitter.com/22lionsbookshop

Instagram.com/22lionsbookshop

Pinterest.com/22lionsbookshop

Introduction

Could you or anyone else change the world? Yes, even though many people can't realize this reality isn't only in what we see but other things too, which lay beyond our eyesight. The easiest level to perceive is the one of our senses: We believe what we see and trust what we hear; we also believe what we feel. And we then think that these ways are all we need to know. But there is another level, below this, in which most people find themselves — the level of illusion, as what happens when we conceive reality according to our mental filters. Most people are not even aware of the idea of reality and what it truly is, or how it works at a vibrational level, much less their capacity to handle it and control it, or even transform it. For this reason, in this book, you will learn about all the levels that compose human consciousness and how to use this information to ascent to a higher state of mind, but also help others achieve the same.

The State of Mass Hypnosis

Why is it that people insist on behaviors that are completely irrational and even refuse to see the negative consequences in their life? In short, the answer is: Mass hypnosis. Most people have been hypnotized by a repetition of concepts, ideas and values, on a daily basis. But how? Quite simply, by exposure: Music, movies, the media, their friends, and their relatives — all of which are exposed to the same.

In school, indoctrination, and peer pressure, reinforces furthermore the idea of the mass opinion as being the most valid. And so, at some point, everyone is full of rationalizations and patterns that are anti-survival. They don't see it, because everyone is under this same hypnotic state. And what controls their rationalizations, in short, are simply lies commonly agreed upon.

This common state of mind is also identified by what is known as being "open-mined". Many so called open-minded individuals, refuse to see how experience proves their values completely wrong, among which is the idea that men and women are the same. They have never been and never will be; men and women choose their partners differently and based on different criteria, betray and cheat for different reasons too, and see life from different angles, valuing different things the most. They also reflect their experiences, failures and emotions, in a different way. To deny such differences means to discriminate them based on gender, because this is what happens with the school system, that denies learning through interaction with objects, and in doing so favors the female gender. If school was a Spartan training academy, we would then be led on the opposite direction, claiming that boys are smarter, more efficient and more effective than girls. And yet, the differentiation itself is made earlier and with more impact at an emotional level, as many studies on psychology have repeatedly shown us, for people always respond according to what is expected from them. Whenever the expectations are higher, they tend to do better.

The attitude of being open-minded leads us then to another, even more naive, state of mind, which is a transe-like state in which people force themselves to believe that the whole world is wonderful, quite often by reinforcing it with mentally devastating meditation techniques, in which they push themselves to repress even more their own emotions. When doing this, such individuals regress to a lower level of immaturity, in which their problems multiply, simply because they can't handle the causes. And the more problems they have that they can't deal with, the further they regress, up to a point in which medication becomes inevitable to handle daily life.

Among the main causes for suffering that people can't handle seeing, is jealousy. It is shocking to admit that many of the people we know, most likely nearly everyone around us, is terribly jealous of our happiness and success, because it accentuates their misery and irresponsibility. And the more miserable and irresponsible someone is, the more this person will resent the success and happiness of others, in relationships, work or simply popularity and attractiveness.

The lack of capacity to handle such truth, brings me to another one that people don't even want to hear: death. We will all die, but somehow, nobody wants to know that. Before death, however, comes change. And so, to admit that our friends change, is to admit that life, as we know it, never remais static and ends too. And this reality — a life in permanent change and transformation towards decadence and death, is unbearable to most humans beings. And so, they remain attached to friends who destroy their relationships, mothers who rejoice in their dramas, and overall, advice that, in the name of "good will" seeks to destroy anything that is good.

How Tyranny is Imposed by the Masses

We don't just die alone; we also fail alone. Everyone is always present to bury us in our dramas and failures before death itself. When we look at human history, we may fail to recognize that no life of a great man or woman was ever self-destroyed on its own, but through the intervention of his or her closest associates. Jealousy has historically been everywhere, although recognizing it is a painful experience that leads us to solitude and separation from those we treasure the most. And yet, it also represents the first stage of awakening.

Apart from jealousy, another element associated with it, and that typically escapes the awareness of those who live in a state of transe, is selfishness. Most people are associated with us only for what we can offer them, either at an emotional, social, financial or sexual level. In other words, families often stick together because they fear loneliness and friends are chosen based on how they make us feel or provide (namely, companionship and access to events and opportunities which we would't see or attend alone), and to a great extent, people associate themselves with us because of our social status or how we can improve their life. That's why the most common questions whenever we meet someone are: "Where are you from?" and "What do you do for a living?"

The "where are you from" reveals your socioeconomic background, which reflects your potential as an individual at a global scale. After all, you have more chances of succeeding in life if you were born in the United States than if you were born in Nigeria. The "what do you for a living" then confirms the previous stereotype true. For you are less likely to succeed when coming from a poor background. But it also ends any possibilities regarding the fact that you might be famous or extraordinary beyond your social stereotype.

The third element people use to judge is your appearance: How you are dressed, how you talk, how you express, and even your tone of voice. Many studies show that more than 80% of our communication is non-verbal. Now, this non-verbal communication may have been subconsciously copied from people you don't even like but spent most of your time with, like an imbecile parent or an arrogant brother; and then you wonder why others don't like you while you talk nicely to them.

As the vast majority of the population is in a zombie-like state of mind, they are not really alive, they are not truly thinking or seeing reality as it is. They are absorbing feelings from appearances and stereotypes, they are judging based on a small set of ideas about the world, and they are constantly matching what they get through their filter of mass-consciousness, which is the same as to say that they think of you as they think of themselves when comparing themselves to the world around them.

The more "open-minded" someone is, the more that person will actually discriminate you based on mass opinion, the more easily this person will betray you based on what others think, and the most likely this person will reveal a competitive mindset that works against you, while pretending to be your friend.

Do you see now, how what seems to be pro-freedom is actually the opposite? Your liberal friends are most likely the type of people you don't want to associate with. But don't take my word for granted, for even I had to go through many years of painful experiences before realizing it — communists, anarchists, socialists, drug addicts, prostitutes, homosexuals, and everyone else in between, betray you and abandon you as easily as you step on a cockroach, and with the same disdain. But I am not against any of these groups, as I was even a strong supporter of some, and the President of various anarchist organizations; I simply learned from direct experience. My open-mindedness today, is conditioned by what I know to be real, and that makes me much more close-minded than I thought I would ever be.

As I said to a friend who is a Freemason and asked for my opinion on homosexuals inside Freemasonry: "I have nothing against homosexuals or their sexual preference and lifestyle, and I also have homosexual friends myself, but I have never met any homosexual who has an energy frequency above what would be considered acceptable, for many of them vibrate at a very low level, and tend to develop other personal issues related to it, namely, promiscuity, alcohol abuse and drug abuse." Many of them, are also demonically possessed, and atheists (which makes them even more vulnerable).

This was confirmed by a homosexual friend who told me the following: "I believe I will never find love because all homosexuals I know and ever met are very promiscuous and not interested in serious relationships."

The same I could say about bisexuals, as they tend to suffer from the same problems that homosexuals do, and are the most likely to cheat on their partners.

How Evil Spreads in the World

We could reduce almost all the fights that there are in the world, and especially the ones we live under our roofs, to the jealousy of others motivating their attacks on our well-being through what they claim to be "friendly advice"; and we could indeed live in peace, if our level of awareness was raised high enough beyond the social filters that remain in between our perceptions and reality itself; or if we put efforts to reach such state through self-education and the reading of books that challenge our views on reality. And this is clearly something that most people don't want to do, reason why they value more fiction than self-development.

Most people want to be distracted from the responsibilities that they can't handle, because they can't grow up — they were never gifted with the tools necessary for their self-development. On the contrary, they were made dependent on authority, first at home, and then through the school system. And so, they remain in an infantile state of mind, consisting of a forced acceptance of their hypnotic state.

When we address the topic of karma, we need to look at this unconsciousness first, because the more one refuses to awaken, the more he or she is likely to fall victim to personal decisions and actions. And for this reason, we could say that karma is a self-imposed punishment.

Truly, a lot of the fights we have with other people, emerge not from what it seems, but from what such people were told in what regards us, or themselves. Fights are always motivated by fear, and fear is motivated by jealousy, which is a distorted view on survival as an individual and part of a collective, as explained before.

If a lot of people attack you and try to separate you from the ones you love, believe me, that it is because you reflect an extremely high social value, otherwise that would never happen. Nobody really cares about the psychopathic boyfriend or girlfriend someone lives with, for example. They usually ask us to be more understanding towards such individual. Because, certainly, the more efforts we put on fixing a broken person, the less time we will have to work on ourselves.

The topic of jealousy and competition eventually becomes shockingly obvious when you realize in due time that all those people either had less than you in what regards to what they were criticizing, or wanted the same and felt arrogantly inferior to you. It is the case of the female friends who say: "Your boyfriend is too ugly for you"; while they themselves are dating a much uglier person; or the ones who say: "You boyfriend is cheating on you"; while the truth is that they would like to cheat with him or have someone as good as him. It is also the scenario of the brother who says to his sister: "Your boyfriend is probably doing something illegal, like selling drugs"; because he himself wants to build his own company and quit his job, but is too stupid to succeed at that, and can't handle the fact that his sister, who he always thought to be dumber than him, found someone better than he will ever be; for it is definitely a strong blow on the ego, when a person who we thought to be inferior to us, wishes to marry someone who will make her life better than ours by association.

All the stories I told you are from real life, and the reason why there are so many, is related to this obsession that human beings on Earth have of imposing their lack of awareness on others and, in doing so, imposing a tyranny of self-destruction.

In the first examples, these women were so obsessed with having a better life than their female friend, that they would rather destroy the relationship. They could't handle the happiness of others because they themselves are not happy. And I saw why, as they were always in fights with their boyfriends and close to ending their own relationships. Making sure that others are in a worse situation, certainly made them feel better with theirs.

The last story is particularly interesting, as we are dealing with arrogance manifesting on a man, which is somehow different from how it shows itself on women. You see, most people don't realize that working independently is much more demanding. You need a lot of self-discipline and more hours of work. Most people can't handle that. They need someone above them to control them. And arrogance is actually a demonstration of weakness, contrary to common belief: The arrogant needs social validation, and you don't get that when you are on your own. That's when arrogance turns against the individual for what it is: fear and weakness. When you are alone, without the possibly of receiving social validation, your fears and weaknesses turn against you, and that's when you are confronted with your real self, the one you had been hiding all these years, by being arrogant and part of the hypnotized masses, doing the exact same thing. You were playing a social game and you don't know it until you are detached from it, i.e., until you don't need to see yourself with your mask on.

That's what weakness truly is: the incapacity to face your own darkness. That's why the arrogant are the most weak people on Earth, and typically the most evil too. For what is evil but fear in disguise. And this is also why all religious books talk about them as the ones who God despises the most. God doesn't like spiritually weak people, because they tend to parasite on others and destroy them intentionally.

The Battle of Good and Evil

The most successful people I ever met are extremely humble. In all areas of life, from the greatest fighters and musicians I ever met, to the best entrepreneurs, all were extremely modest and friendly. But you can't fake humbleness. You naturally become humble when you are only competing against yourself. What others think becomes less important at that point, and that's how arrogance vanishes from you.

Arrogant people are weak, because they need social validation to feel important. And as long as you are competing with the outside world for validation, you are not competing with yourself but instead ignoring your real self. That is why people who are obsessed with how others view them, have no idea of what to do with their own life.

Narcissists, despite their grandiose sense of entitlement, for example, are, ironically, always lost in life. Their goals are only directed at what gives them social validation, quite commonly towards more money, even if that implies prostituting themselves to a job they hate, ideas that violate their moral, or literally speaking, as in the case of many models, who use social media for that purpose, and to attract a rich husband.

The paradox on everyone that wants to compete at a higher level, is that they need to improve themselves to be able to do that, and that competition with themselves, with becoming better, makes them humble by default.

That's why I know that the man from that story above will never succeed in life. He is obsessed with how others see him, and that conflicts with who he is. He can't do both things at the same time, focusing on the outside and the inside at the same time. You either do what you must or what others approve. One part of him wants to buy a house to impress his friends and family, and another part of him is afraid that he will not be able to afford it, if working independently.

These stories become even more interesting when you expand them to look at those associated with them. His girlfriend, for example, is seeing a psychologist, which makes me believe she was fooled into thinking she is the one with mental problems. It's very common for the victim of a Narcissist to think that, which is probably the case here as well. He is projecting at her who he is, just as he projects his hatred at those who have what he can't get.

Now, that's arrogance and weakness at the highest levels, and that's why the arrogant are so concerned about looking like they are better than you and anyone else. If the mask fell from their face, and you saw them for who they really are, you would probably feel sorry for them.

I have seen that many times; it is like watching a little child pretending to be king. And in indeed it is, for they are representing childlike attitudes, through years of investment on the game of pretending.

You see, they never grew up. They only learn to pretend to be accepted by others. And quite commonly, if you keep on expanding this awareness, you will see that they copied their distorted models from their own family, who does the same.

As psychologists say, the ones who should visit them, almost never do. It is usually the ones who don't need, who do that. And so, that naive girlfriend of his, is reading books on relationships, and seeing a psychologist, because she truly believes her relationship is collapsing because of her, and not the arrogant imbecile she lives with. She was fooled by the mask. And that's how many are fooled too. She may read all the books she can find and spend years on a psychologist, never seeing this truth. In fact, seeing it, would mean the end of her relationship as well, so she most likely doesn't want it either. And here we have another paradox so commonly represented in our world: The healthy ones trying to improve themselves to help the unhealthy, and the unhealthy pulling the healthy ones down at the same time; One group competing for the well-being of another group, who wishes only to destroy everyone in the process, including themselves.

What Ignorance Looks Like

There are different words to describe the same: Ignorant, stupid, obnoxious, rude; and there will always be many concepts to apply on the same things, because we see that a lot, and we need words to describe what we see. But where is this reality coming from? Where are these behaviors coming from? I will tell you: What we describe as ignorant is basically a person who does not know, does not read, does not care, and is misinformed, and also a person who cannot process information or learn. Because, you see, many times, the ignorant is the one believing that he is smarter than others.

When the fool wishes to teach the wise, and the wise refuses to agree with the fool, the fool always assumes that the wise is arrogant, therefore projecting and justifying the foolishness at the same time and in the best way possible. In mirroring himself with his conclusions, the fool then remains satisfied for who he is, and in doing so, keeps the level of consciousness he is capable of assimilating.

When someone tells me that I don't know what's happening in the world, for example, and I ask back why they say that, they usually then answer something like: "Well, because I saw in the news this, and that and so on". Many times what they're describing me is false, and I know because I am informed enough too; On the other hand, many times what they describe me is totally illogical as well; and so, after a few hours of research, I can easily discredit everything they say and believe to be true. And yet, they keep on believing that they're better informed than me, because they believe that their source is correct. And so, as you can understand, there are different types of ignorance.

A poor person is not necessarily ignorant. He is merely trying to survive with scarce means. Many would access knowledge if offered. But there are people who indeed choose to be ignorant, because they associate knowledge with complexity and confusion. They themselves have been confused so many times, by so many ignorant intellectuals, that they learned to depreciate books and information. And when I ask them if they read any books, they usually will say something like: "I was reading some books in school and that is all".

I then may ask them: Did you like those books? What kind of book were? And well, when they describe the books, I can understand that the books were boring, maybe too old as well, and we don't speak like Shakespeare anymore, and so, what this creates in people's mind is a lack of motivation for learning, which they then carry on with themselves throughout their whole existence. Many followers of the bible, for example, are actually in this state of mind. Their thinking can't handle more than one book and compare information from different sources. If they could do that, they could call themselves members of a religious congregation. But because they can't, we have no name them cult members.

Moreover, if from an early age, people are demotivated, they don't have incentives later in life to pick books, especially if they have much less time available. This is something which a reader discovers by himself, and discovers because he is curious. For the majority do not associate need with knowledge. They say that they need money but won't learn how to obtain it. They say that they need a better relationship, but don't want to learn how to create one. They say that they need a better world, but don't really want to do anything to have one. They even say that they wish to change their life, but meanwhile, they're learning nothing to make that change occur. And sometimes people wish they had more friends too, they wish to be married, wish to have their own family, but aren't doing anything to obtain all of that as well.

Eventually, emerges a more interesting side from the spectrum of that reality, which is the one they can't see. Because when people are too immersed in their own suffering, their own ignorance, they can't even see that the problems they create return back at them. And so, when people fail, for example, in relationships, they tend to always believe that the next one will be the right one, that the next one is better and out there, waiting for them, that the real person who will love them for who they are, is waiting somewhere. They believe the same when failing in all their friendships. They never think for a moment that it might be their fault. They think that it's always someone else's fault. And so, we have here ignorance associated with irresponsibility, but also a low level of consciousness, because indeed the ignorant is not conscious of his own ignorance, and that's what makes him ignorant in the first place.

What Self-Development Should Be

What happens with the ignorant is that he or she can't perceive personal responsibility, or even lack of knowledge. And so, we can say that these elements are always present at a relatively similar level: Intelligence, responsibility and consciousness. And these three scales of measurement reveal another one, even more important: mental health.

Humanity only gets confused about this, because these four concepts have never been properly described, but rather relativized. But to avoid any more doubts, here is the real meaning of these four concepts and the most clear explanation you will ever find:

- **Intelligence:** The ability to adapt to different situations at a mental, emotional and physical level. It includes the capacity to learn abstract concepts like numbers and words; the capacity to process emotions and feel empathy for others, or to be emotionally intelligent; and the capacity to learn with the body, namely, with sports, dancing, martial arts, or in playing musical instruments, and other ways that imply physical coordination;

- **Responsibility:** The capacity to take fault or to see the implications of one's behaviors on others and his own life. It is also the capacity to learn and take actions towards what one desires to achieve;

- **Consciousness:** The capacity to see the world as one, connected at different levels, namely, the spiritual, the subconscious and the conscious. It is also the capacity to differentiate all those levels with different forms of life and from different perspectives;

- **Mental Health:** The capacity to process similarities and differences between people and elements of reality in an effective way. The fool never produces the results he wishes to accomplish; and obviously, the most extreme example of this, would be to talk to someone who isn't there, or to see things that aren't real. But as we progress up this scale, we will notice other, less obvious form of delusion, like projecting imaginary characteristics on someone who doesn't have them, or making conclusions during conversations based on personal assumptions. And at this point, surely, you can see how insane almost everyone on this planet is.

Until we address these four elements as I mentioned here, there is no hope for Earth. And if you want to evaluate the spiritual level of any human being, you can use these four elements as described to do that, for you will obtain an accurate result that will never fool you in predicting their behaviors, their intentions, and even their future.

You can always expect failure from the lower stages of this scale. They fail at all levels, and tend to suffer too, from the consequences of their own failures.

In those who present a higher state of potential or awareness, you will see the opposite, for they tend to succeed against all expectations and many times even against their opportunities. The physical world seems to bend to their needs. Because when a person is evolved enough, that person also emanates a higher energy, which attracts similar energy in vibration, while repelling opposing energy. When they focus on something, they get it faster than anyone else, and they also manage it better when achieving it. For this reason, these individuals are the most grateful too.

One of the interesting aspects of the empaths, for example, is that they are highly appreciative of everything and everyone that does something for them. They are very humble and grateful. And so, due to these same reasons, they are typically perceived as weak and vulnerable. And yet, they also demonstrate these four elements at the highest level: When you are more evolved, you are also, and naturally, more sensitive and more kind.

The price such people pay for their higher level comes in the form of self-hatred, whenever they can't defend themselves against the evilness of the world and express their anger precisely and in the right moments. When doing that, however, the masses rapidly change their view on them from naive to being crazy. But they are not insane; they are just misaligned with the rest of the planet.

They are the forefront of evolution and should be treasured as the best religious leaders, teachers and gurus, by those who seek to know more.

The Planetary Barrier Towards Higher Realms

Many people ask me how do I know so much. And well, I know because I have curiosity and the need to understand the world around me. In fact, I was many times criticized for asking too many questions; but how am I supposed to learn if I do not and cannot ask questions? And then there's this idea, in many countries around the world, that the one who asks questions, is the one who is ignorant, while the one who asks nothing is smart. And that's a completely wrong assumption. The most ignorant people I ever met, are also the most arrogant I know. Their ignorance comes from arrogance. They believe to know enough and that their values are good enough, and so, they trap themselves in a mindset that doesn't allow seeing their own mistakes and weaknesses. Their thinking patterns become reduced to the vast number of repetitions they live with and see others living with. Because of that, they attribute any illogical event to the fault of elements alien to their reality. It's like walking around the house and dropping a glass on the floor, and saying that the glass broke, and therefore someone else did it; the "me" part becomes separated from the ego.

As the ego is one of the layers of the self, the one in between the outside world and the perception we make of it, such people end up separating responsibility from their own true self, and then saying: "I want this and someone else has to provide it for me". It is entitlement rooted on a complete disregard for responsibility over the mechanics of one's own life, i.e., immaturity. The ignorant have arrogance and a strong belief in their own entitlement, like a kindergarten bully who was never thought how to behave properly.

The dependence on external elements that one wishes to selfishly use to withdraw resources to his own life, roots him in his confidence on himself, despite having no value whatsoever backing such beliefs. And that's why entitlement comes also from a misalignment of values, or crisis in personal values, quite often emerging from a social crisis in human values. People are led to believe the wrong things, and then spend a lifetime trying to force those things to work. It's like being hypnotized into being someone else and then spending his entire time explaining to the hypnotizer that his name is not "Samuel" but "Samantha". Have you ever watched that? You should. Because shows on hypnotism describe us, through a small sample, how the rest of the world is. The audience on those shows, clapping and laughing, is unaware that they themselves will spend an entire lifetime role-playing hypnotic suggestions, most of which obtained during childhood.

Ignorance then becomes explained as an attempt at justifying the unreal with beliefs one insists on living by, due to hypnotic suggestions and a transe-like mentality.

The dependence on external elements dissociated from a knowing of the self, portrayed in dogs who don't know they are dogs, but believe to be humans, and are even scared of other dogs, or of seeing themselves in the mirror, is also a perfect example of how most people live. They react in the same way when confronted with the truth about themselves — the social mirror. And there's nothing better than relationships to show them exactly that. Because if someone in a relationship tells you that you are fat, ugly, old and rude, that person, no matter how imbecile and rude may be, is mirroring at you the reflection you project on others.

We may either like or dislike it, accept or feel sad, and develop self-hatred with what we project on others, but we can't deny that reality without being delusional first. And the best example of what I am telling you, comes in the recording of your own voice.

So many times I have asked myself why people stop buying my books once they hear my voice, or why I struggle to explain myself to those who know me; and eventually, once I listened to my voice, I understood why. It did not sound like what I was perceiving in my brain. I did not had a tone of confidence and strength, because I was not trying to convince people. I was expecting others to trust me based on the information I was sharing, and I was being naive in doing that, because that's not how human beings judge information. People are sensitive to their perceptions and they don't qualify something as good or bad, before those perceptions validate the information. In other words, a gentle tone of voice discredited anything I could say.

This understanding led me to another conclusion about how humans function: People judge not by what is logic, but what sounds credible to them. Human beings completely disregard the truth because they lack the capacity to reach it. And that's how I realized I am not so human as I thought I was, as I actually possess the skills to process information up to a very high level of validity.

Most people can't do that. They remain in the realm of appearances, comparing and judging based on what they validate on that realm, supported by social perceptions. In other words, most people are stuck, no matter how smart they think they are, or how scientific they want to be, on the global level of consciousness, and can't go independently beyond it. And so, it does not make any sense to talk about enlightenment before we address the mass consciousness barrier in which the whole planet is submerged. A person will never understand and much less reach enlightenment before crossing this barrier.

Why Altruism is Rejected by the Majority

The world we have today, may not be perfect for us but it is certainly much better than it ever was. And I wish three hundred years ago people had access to the internet and free books as they have today. I wish they had access to podcasts too, so they could learn every day and grow. And yet, during those times, they struggled even to go to school. There weren't so many libraries as what we have today, or so many bookstores.

Indeed, we have come a long way in order to build a better society. But our society of today isn't good enough yet. And the ignorant can't see this. They are trapped in the consciousness of the masses, due to their subconscious limitations, mostly composed of the fear of rejection and the need for approval. These two poles keep people's thoughts conditioned within mass consciousness, vibrating at the same frequency as everyone else, and absorbing the similar thoughts that vibrate under this same frequency.

This said, how is it possible to be more patient with the ignorant? The first step would be by understanding them. And I have just showed you how. If you know why they are ignorant and what makes a person ignorant, you will actually start feeling pity and compassion for them, and then understand why they will never be able to understand someone that is outside their paradigms. In fact, any person that those, trapped in mass consciousness, come in contact with, will inevitably be placed in one of those three areas of the brain: Validation (i.e., perceived value in accordance to the pyramid structure of society), fear (i.e., unacceptable social behaviors or politically incorrect behaviors that categorize someone immediately as a threat), and equality (i.e., behaviors, thoughts and beliefs that equalize mass consciousness).

In other words, the need for equality in the world feeds on the fear or terror towards the unknown and a deep desire for belonging and social validation, to be accepted and respected, despite any immoral and unethical actions that one may have. Fear is the cause of bullying and the reason why people discriminate others, which increases when they feel that their world is being threatened by the differences perceived around them, quite often promoted and accentuated by mass media. And validation, often placed on monetary acquisitions, leads people to disregard everything else that makes them a better person, including ethical behavior. In fact, ethics, when applied as an act of rebellion against a majority, is considered an unacceptable behavior that promotes fear, and in doin so, stimulates hatred. That's why the most ethical people in the world have always been condemned and discriminated by the masses.

On the other hand, the ignorant always suffer the consequences of their behaviors, throughout their entire life, and even while not seeing it, while not seeing themselves causing their own misfortune. The ignorant won't grow, expand or become wiser. And like so, won't become richer and happier too. And because they are arrogant, to compensate for this refusal in introspecting themselves, to match mass consciousness in their ignorance, and despite their frustration, they will always follow the masses in picking scapegoats to blame.

The ignorant are more prone to commit crimes, precisely because of this belief in entitlement. If an ignorant person believes that he is entitled to get things that he isn't receiving, he can commit a crime more easily than anyone else to get it. And that's how the ignorant masses have always been deceived into supporting revolutions against those in power, which very often, replaced that power for a more oppressive one. That was the case of the French Revolution which led to the tyranny of Napoleon Bonaparte, and the Russian Revolution, which gave rise to the Soviet Union.

Why Ignorance Leads to Oppression

The incapacity to perceive the implications or long term consequences of one's actions on himself and others, is exactly what makes a person ignorant. And that's why the ignorant are also more punished by society, and much more than anyone else who understands law, community rights and human rights.

The ignorant are also more prone to divorce, more prone to be abused, and the ignorant are also abused by other ignorant people as well. For the ignorant always identities the most with other ignorant people like them. The ignorant don't like people who know more, therefore, they feel more attracted to people who know less than them. And those who know less than them, give them a sense of reasoning that is not there, and feed their ego; and while doing this, supporting a worse state of mind — a lower consciousness. In other words, the more ignorant someone is, the more suffering he gets; and the more egotism he possesses, the more prone to betrayal he is, and the more damage he makes on his own life because of the thoughts and views of others; and the more betrayal one obtains, the more reinforced his beliefs in his delusional self are, and the more he feels to be morally just to commit crimes; and the more crimes he commits, the more lack of trust he gets; and the more lack of trust he gets, the more lack of love he has, and the more unhappiness he gives back, and receives, and on and on; and so, their existence becomes a downward spiral towards the end.

It is not illogical to assume that stupidity quite often breeds lack of empathy, and this lack of empathy is preyed upon by Narcissistic Individuals, who get their power over the masses by exploiting such weakness. And so, it's not illogical to say as well, that a Narcissist, motivated by a desire for power, and reverence, will always lead the sheep majority towards its own destruction. That's why evil always corrupts with the selfishness within every human being.

It is up to each person to make a decision towards satisfying that desire to prey on the innocent by following the corrupt majority, or to make a turn sideways, and face the consequences of being different.

The courage to move independently from a group is always a divine act, motivated by ethics and validated by God only. Humans rarely perceive independence and courage as an act of spiritual advancement towards a higher moral.

Despite this, many people ask: "What could I have done?" They ask this because they tend to victimize themselves when cornered, when pushed towards responsibility; and that's why they then say: "I had no chance in life." And, well, that's not true. You always have a chance in life, which is to ignore the potential outcome of going on a certain way and acting in a certain way. Many times you have chances offered by life, and you ignore every single one of them; and that's a choice too.

People don't lose all their moral and ethics in one day, or decision, as much as they don't lose their spirit to the dark side in the same manner. This process takes time and is gradual. Step by step, everyone is either going towards a higher good or a darker evil. And you can actually analyze their steps to see in which direction they are heading.

The Decision to Change Oneself

I was ignorant in my life as well and I can't say I was lucky. But I could have blamed my family and background, the country where I was born, the city, and I did not. Instead, I simply felt sad with the whole situation. I was surrounded by ignorant people, but life gave me opportunities, and step by step, life brought me to where I am today, far from all that reality, and so far that nobody who met me when I was a child, even believed that I would become a writer one day, much less doing podcasts, speaking in public, or changing the world. That part of changing the world was certainly and completely out of their imagination, as much or more than talking about UFOs. But I could not have done all that by myself. The first step happened with what I call Earth Angels, you know, people who come to your life while not knowing who you are, and giving you a chance to move far from your situation. And it doesn't matter how they are dressed or what they say; it only matters their intention. I don't even care about their background. Again, what matters is their intention; and many of them were religious. But that was, nonetheless, my first step — to be among religious people who have good intentions. And it doesn't matter also what kind of book or religion it was, because I was indeed with people from different religions. I embraced them all: I was with Christians, Buddhists, Hindus, Scientologists, Rosicrucians, Freemasons, and more; and saw all those steps as a blessing from God. And yet, I also noticed that while they were guiding me somewhere, contrary to the belief of the members of these groups, they were guiding me towards my real self, and not the membership of their group.

At the same time, I was offered opportunities in the form of books that I found or that were offered to me through those congregations and the people I met there. And even though I did not earn much, I was working part-time hours in many jobs just to be able to afford those books.

Many of the jobs I had, where indeed just to pay for those books. And I was spending more time and money investing on my books, the spiritual knowledge to change myself, rather than, even, at some point in my life, studying for my college degree. I was spending more days of the week reading the books I bought, than studying for exams. And I sacrificed even my grades, my hours of sleep (and I was sleeping an average of 3 to 4 hours a day), but I was welcoming all of those sacrifices. Because you need to work with what is given to you and appreciate everything as God's blessing and answers to your prayers. If you don't have enough time, then you must give more time. If you don't have enough money, you must invest more money on your purpose. But you need to work with what is given to you. You can't expect, all of your life, to get something else or more without giving back in return, in time, efforts, money, and anything else that is required from you to prove your faith.

Eventually, one concept connected to another, and another, and I started realizing many things which I never even considered to be possible. I started learning secrets about life, which completely changed my perspective of it. Many answers would even be completed during my sleep, in the form of dreams. And yet, true wisdom starts with a decision. You can decide that life is responsible for what occurs to you, or you are responsible for what happens to your life. And so, being ignorant is actually to refuse responsibility, i.e., a choice.

Nowadays, there is even something I did not have when I was younger, which is thousands and thousands of books at the distance of our pocket, in the form of ebooks we can download to our mobile. Instead of wasting time with the internet, people can actually go on libraries to read free books too that will make them a better a person. They simply don't have the habit and that's why they don't do this. And that's why ignorance is today, more than ever, a choice.

What Can We Expect From Others

We can't change people, and make them read, until they feel the necessity to do so. And that comes in the form of empathy: the need to understand what others feel, think and see. We can inspire that attitude in others by asking: "What do you think that person feels when you say such things?" And we can turn all problems in the world to the same topic: Lack of empathy.

Lack of empathy is ignorance; and there are indeed different levels and types of ignorance. There is the ignorance of the mind, the ignorance of the heart, and there is the ignorance of the spirit as well. And people suffer from different types of ignorance.

You can see these things more clearly when addressing a child's education. If you show a child how good it is to be a good person, and you teach this child about the wisdom of the mind, the wisdom of the heart, and the wisdom of the spirit, the child will appreciate all this and embrace it as his or her own knowledge.

The wisdom of the mind, can be applied by taking a child to a library, and helping him or her study, read and learn. The wisdom of the heart, is about teaching the child how good we feel when giving back to society. And this includes, for example, telling a child to give money to a poor person in the street. And then, the wisdom of the spirit regards the benefits that a child may not even know if not shown. And this spiritual aspect, for some, means taking a child to church, or making her read spiritual books, or even study a religious book. But spirituality is basically life itself.

So what's the difference between teaching a child about the heart, the mind, or the spirit? The qualities of the spirit are personal, and yet, they're connected to our relation with the cosmos; all forms of depression and unhappiness, in general, come from such disconnection, with the planet, others, love, and ourselves — our true self. If you teach a child to embrace all that, and to love the planet, she will understand spirituality much better than most adults.

This said, how do we change other people, namely, adults, or even ourselves? And is such change even possible?

For that we need to look first at the structure of our spiritual identity, and only then, the identity of others will make sense to us. We are composed, fundamentally, of three elements: Our mind, our heart and our desires. And whenever one of these elements is being ignored, we can't truly change ourselves or others. These things may be present at different moments, with more intensity in one or another, depending on the motivations of a person. And so, we must address our spiritual seeds as a form of momentary need for change. A seed, in this case, is your purpose — a conscious guidance filled with desire. And is this purpose honest? Is the person communicating it honestly? Because if the purpose is honest and the communication is effective, this seed will be planted. And here's a brutal example of such truth: When we get angry at someone, and then speak the truth, that person may not like it and not speak to us again. But they will certainly remember our words for a long time. And they will likely take those words into consideration in their lifetime; maybe even forever.

When you plant such seeds, you lose the plant; nothing remains the same and people leave your life. So a big part of this honesty towards others is also related to yourself. Because, you see, if you're afraid to lose someone, because you told him or her the truth, then you're not being honest. Full honesty demands an absence of ego, and when you let go of the ego, you then let go of the fears attached to the ego, and that means that whatever comes, will come; and you are then only focused on what you're saying and doing. But if the seed you're putting out, has no ego and no personal desire, and is pure honesty, and applied with altruism, well then, the impact will be huge too. Because, you see, when people ask me how to change the world, or accept that nobody can, they are expressing a belief either way. And yet, without being arrogant, I can clearly say that I am changing the world. My purpose is not to change the world, for if that was my purpose, I would not be able to change it. My purpose is to help others. And that's altruism: Heart, mind and desire, was what made it possible.

Nevertheless, many times, when you help people, they become worse than they were: more fearful or simply better at betraying others, lying and deceiving. So you can't truly predict how a change, even when good, will impact another being. On the other hand, when people don't want to change, it is because they can't.

I've been with people who wanted to change, and even asked me for help to change themselves, but they couldn't handle such changes, and for that reason, I know that, to my sadness, they won't overcome their karma in this lifetime; maybe not even in the next one.

Why People Repeat Their Problems

Many times, when people repeat the same problems, the process blocks their development, as they become frozen on the traumas and the pain accumulated from suffering repeatedly. Many people do seem to grow beyond their problems and challenges, but these issues affect them in different ways. Some people can suffer all of their life, because of what was said to them in the past, and damaged their self-esteem. And the reason why they can't change is because they are sick, trapped inside their own pain, unable to reach such level of consciousness, which they have segregated into their subconscious mind in the form of suppression. And this is why one of the most efficient ways to change someone, is by loving them, even though not everyone can be loved. Many people give back pain because they can't accept love and never will.

Sometimes, you also can love someone more, by not changing that person. I know because I've seen this occurring many times. When I notice that a person can't be changed, because of her personality, her words, or the way she reacts to something, I then do something else, and choose to love this person from the distance. And when this happens, usually, the person will voluntarily want a change. Because many times what such individuals need is just love and acceptance. And once they find it, they become motivated to change.

I've worked with people in different scenarios, including with children suffering from learning disabilities, and one thing I did, that made everyone, parents and teachers, angry, was that I would ignore their exams, requests and grades, and instead, whenever seeing the child, focus only on that child, while ignoring everything such people said. In fact, as I would find quite often, many of them were completely deluded about the child, with no idea about his or her true identity. And so, what I did in many of these situations, was to simply sit next to the child and let him or her speak. I would not even control the conversation, but just let them speak, and ask simple questions about their life, and what they like to do. And you know, these children don't have experience with such interactions, as they are not used to be respected. Therefore, when they notice that they're being respected by an adult, they start talking in a completely different way; they start expressing more, asking more questions; and when feeling that you're truly listening to them, when they feel that you really care about what they say, they then continue to express even more, and at some point, when the awareness of who they are expands, the traps within their soul are revealed; at some point, they will talk about how what their family says is affecting them; and quite often, they have parents and other people, such as their own teachers, with very low expectations on them. For some reason, they are seen as ignorant, and obviously, their grades reinforce that stigma.

This leads me to the solution, as the first thing I do, is to create a plausible doubt on the child: "Are you sure you are ignorant? Could you allow me to prove that assumption wrong?" And you see, nobody likes to be stupid. So obviously, such children want to be wrong in what regards this belief. On the other hand, the same doesn't occur with adults. With adults, I noticed that it's much more difficult to apply this process. They typically say: "I can't achieve this" or "I can't achieve that" or even "I don't deserve that". And sometimes, I try to create a doubt in them: "What if you deserved it?" But that possibility is only exciting for children. It is very scary for adults. Most adults are scared of changing, even when they know it will make them better and improve their life. Change in an adult represents restarting, relearning, reforming one's identity, and worse than all that, the assumption that one was wrong, which is delimited by the power of the ego over oneself.

How the Ego Nullifies Awareness

Stupidity isn't really a problem or a state of being. Sometimes I tell people that they are acting stupid, and they get offended, but it's just a word describing behaviors. So what actually offends them is the possibility of being wrong, and that's arrogance. People are easily offended because they are narcissists to a certain extent. When they then call me stupid in return, in order to offend me, they prove this to be true. But I don't really get offended, because I know what I know and what I don't know. If I don't know something and someone calls me stupid because of that, I don't really care. I even admit that I am indeed stupid on many topics, as I have done in public many times. But they are then surprised by the fact that my ego isn't there to collect the pain, because that's their real intention when using such words, which, again, reflects their own personal challenges — they are blinded by the ego, trapped in a childlike mindset; and that state deceives their awareness to the meaning of my words and intention, which emerge from a higher level, beyond their capacity to comprehend.

We can't know everything but we can have the desire to learn and change and that's where everything starts. And so, not all seeds can be planted on all grounds. We must first know if a ground is fertile enough before a seed can be planted there. And most people are not fertile enough for a change or opportunity to be planted in them; because their mind is already corrupted by many wrong ideas — their ego poisons their awareness.

Moreover, and Interestingly enough, the most common insult I receive from others is "arrogance"; because people tend to reflect at others their own denied emotions, which in this case is jealousy. People suffer because of their decisions, and that awareness becomes even more unbearable when they believe to be following the right religion, the right practices, the right mindset, and even associating themselves with those they consider to be the right people. It is surely hard when God comes and says: You are wrong.

Fortunately for them, God is not in physical form to show them that; but He shows Himself in many other ways, that they deny seeing; and one who has his head stuck on one book, often neglects, on purpose, all those ways. It is easier to be religious with one book only than with many, but also more delusional.

The last time I was called arrogant, showed me this same pattern. First, a friend who is a member of the religion called Jehovah Witnesses, asked me for one of my books, and I offered him one of the latest, about money. Apparently, he got very offended with the content and did not even try to finish it. But soon after that, decided to lecture me on how money is evil and corrupts people. During all his time, however, in which he was laughing at my answers, assuming to know more than me, and trying to prove me wrong with biblical quotes, he was calling from a room in Ukraine that he was sharing with six other people. And I must say, it is very pathetic, when a man with more than forty years old can't afford his own apartment but needs to share it with six other people, and yet, believes that he can lecture me on money. Because, not only he can't, but is also showing me that he should quit his religion and become one of my disciples instead. At least, last time I was in Ukraine, I rent a whole apartment for myself, even if I was eating out every day, and never at home.

I always rent apartments wherever I go. I find it humiliating to have to share the same space where I sleep or eat with a stranger. I am also not interested in wasting my time in trying to make myself look pleasant in the house of someone else. I simply pay for the space and take it. And why I can do that? Because I worked very hard to obtain the life I have now. But even on what regards this topic, he had to attack with stupidity, telling me that working hard is not a spiritual thing to do and not the right way to live. And I must say, regarding such belief, that it is very sad to realize that this man has been a Jehovah Witness all of his life, and can't even find a woman inside his own congregation to marry him. He has been traveling the whole world, including South America, Europe and even Russia and the Middle East, trying to find a wife in as many countries as possible, and no woman from his own group wants him, because he is indeed pathetic, and the fact that the women he meets are from his own religious group doesn't change that truth. In fact, women from the Jehovah Witness, as I have often noticed in many countries where I was invited to attend their meetings, are so demanding, that they will gladly marry someone living in a different country and even change country, just to make sure that they're getting the best among the best.

I think that many men join this group believing that they will have an easier life, but not even their prayers are listened, for most of them end up single for many years. Many struggle financially too because of their stupid views on the bible.

The same I could say about Scientologists, who claim to know a lot about money, sell courses on money, give seminars on money, but are all poor, and constantly extorting money from the rich. A Scientologist will love you only for as long as you have money to pay back for studies. When you can't, they forget you as if you were just a pet rock.

I did ask them often a question that none was able to answer: "You repeat that money is not important, but you want me to pay for courses that cost thousands of dollars. Does that mean I can pay you with hugs and kisses?"

The most insulting behavior of Scientologists that I have personally experienced was certainly to persuade me to give them data on my bank account while analyzing my answers to see how much I could pay them. In the name of help, they apply extortion on their members, and yet, they say that only suppressive people pervert help. They are the perverts and the suppressives themselves that they claim to fight against, and as much as the Jehovah Witness and many christian-obsessed groups are more satanic than God Himself would like to admit.

Many of these religions are infected with many Narcissists, and Narcissistic Personality Disorder is just a psychiatric term for Demonic Possession. But one doesn't need to believe these words, for anyone can take their own teachings to mirror their actions. Every single time I used a bible of the Jehovah Witness to show them how much God hates their actions, and is in total contradiction, or took quotes from L. Ron Hubbard's books to show to Scientologists that they contradict what they claim do defend, such people always stopped talking to me and disappeared completely, no matter for how many years I have met them, or how many times they have repeated to me the words: "I am your friend and you can trust me". Truly, they can't even trust themselves, and I need to trust lunatics that have no idea of what they're doing.

Does this mean that psychologists or psychiatrists are better options to a completely lost world? Certainly not, because worse than people with mental problems trying to help other people with mental problems, is these same people lacking in moral and ethical behavior as well. The ones I know who claim to be helped by psychiatrists end up addicted to antidepressants, and develop a higher sensibility to self-analysis and introspection, which makes them push away people who truly care for them. The ones who go on psychologists tend to end up with a lower self-esteem than when they arrived there the first time. But how can one feel good when a psychologist says, as one said to one of my friends: "It is normal to have suicidal thoughts but if it happens again, call me before you kill yourself."

What was this woman implying? That she can help in choosing the least painful way to commit suicide? And how can people protect themselves against diabolical psychologists like these ones? Compared to any religion out there, psychology and psychiatry have done more destruction in a few decades, that all religions combined in thousands of years. And despite all that, they still don't know anything significant about the human mind.

As someone once said, the imbecile of this world inspire us to do better. Because if any moron can create a religion or therapy and represent that as an authority, then someone that can see all of these things has the moral duty to create his own path. And maybe these are God's signs that I should start my own. My awareness has certainly surpassed their ego and mental structure to realize their own limitations, more than my own. And that certainly puts my work on a very high level of quality.

The Energies That Shape Our Experiences

Another interesting fact about these and many other religions, is how much they admire me and say that I represent everything they defend, but quickly change their mind when I reject them and accuse them of blasphemy. Surely, if they met God in person and the same occurred, they would then claim that He isn't their God, and would call Satan to their true God. That is why Nietzsche was right when saying that God is dead and is nothing more than Man's invention. But the real God is not dead. Nietzsche's God is the God of humanity and that God is indeed dead. It lives only in the imaginary of the collective. We know that by the fact that every single atheist manifests demonic possession whenever confronted with an enlightened being. And you can't have demons without a God. Every exorcist gets their faith reestablished by experience if they ever had any doubt about it.

Atheists empty themselves from any spiritual resistance that could deny the possession of their mind. They become empty vessels to be used when needed. That is why whenever we see a crowd of people in protest, they seem to go wild and act in irrational ways, that they later can't explain. It's not the energy of the group that makes them do what they do, but rather their low vibrational state that invited possession unto them.

We are often subjected to the energies that lay within us and around us. The same thing applies to countries. You won't prosper everywhere. Every land and every city has its own energy, which fits a particular moment in your life. In some places, for example, I am appreciated and loved, while in others I am hated and discriminated, while being the exact same individual.

Also, so many people tell me that nobody ever offered them books, not even relatives or friends, and yet, there are people to whom you offer a book, and they won't read or say: "Thank you". Many people even judge before reading, by saying: "I don't read such things"; or "I don't believe in those books". Moreover, there are people with whom I spent hours in helping them, who do not even say: "thank you". Isn't this incredible? Why should God help them? Worse than that, is the vast amount of people who waste money on beers and fancy dinners with friends, but ask me for books for free? Do I spend entire days working and writing because I am stupid and have nothing better to do with my time? In some of these cases, I did offer them what they wanted out of compassion, and sometimes even more than twenty books, and as a result of that, they would insult me, saying later that the books don't match me as a person. And so, as you see, most people don't deserve to be helped. They complain about their problems, but deserve the problems they have. Some people also create the problems they have in their life and they like them too, because the problems justify their own hell. And they prove, with such actions, that the way out of hell is by burning inside of it. That burning is found in the growing, in becoming more self-sufficient and responsive and compassionate.

As you can now see, many of those who live in hell, deserve it, for lack of empathy. They created their own problems. But we don't have to be responsible for the problems others create for themselves. We can offer them help, but if they disrespect it and keep going nowhere, in circles, then it's time to let them go. As I said to a friend who wishes to change the world: If you truly wish to change the world, you must also know that this same world will never appreciate you.

How to Change the World

Once the world becomes like you, you aren't important to this world anymore. For when you create changes in this reality, which reality then reflects back at you, the reflection and you become the same. And that means, by definition, that you're not important any longer.

Those who want to be important will never change the world, because they want the world to admire them, and for that to occur, the world needs first to be at their level and not overcome it. In other words, they're not being effective even though able to receive admiration. If you are truly effective, you always lose attention by differentiation. If you are effective, the world also, most likely, won't even see you, or it will absorb you instead. Whenever I help people and change them completely, and they learn a lot from me in the process, they become super fast in their life but they then don't need me anymore, and suddenly, I become just another human being in their reality. And yet, when they met me, they treated me as if I was a god.

After being helped and many times, people don't even show respect. And this is something that, when you're effective, you need to live with, as most people won't appreciate you. There are actually people that I know, who steal my words, without ever quoting me, and then do public speakings with thousands of listeners and help nobody, because they are focused on themselves only — their own ego. But after one thousand years have passed, everyone alive today will be dead, and the only thing that will remain, are the changes we created in the world; and so, this is what you need to consider: What is the legacy you wish to leave behind? Because, even those who steal from you today to feed their ego, are doing God's work, for they spread your message in their name but the message was not even yours to begin with — Truth is universal. Even if the wrong individuals are praised after the death of the real geniuses, that doesn't change the outcome.

For example, Nikola Tesla doesn't appear in history books, but the one who stole his knowledge and slandered his reputation does, i.e., Thomas Edison. Nikola Tesla wanted a world in which energy was freely accessible from the Earth itself, and what a difference that would make on the whole planet: Economies would be more equalitarian, there would be no pyramid structure of power, and most likely, the United States and Great Britain wouldn't have the political influence they have today. Many wars would not even be fought or would be won by other, unexpected parties, and we would all be much more prosperous. Technology could be much more advanced too. But what kind of humans would live in such world? I can only assume that humanity was not and is not yet prepared for the level of spirituality that a huge advancement on technology and resources would bring. We can see this in how most people perceive empathy or help.

You must know that, when helping someone, you help the whole planet too. If you consider that such person will die, you need to consider too if you're helping a selfish soul or someone that can multiply that help and love to bring more good to others. You should never help the selfish, greedy and egotistical. The planet depends on such energy not being wasted, in order to be made effective. And if we believe in reincarnation, our level of responsibility is even higher, for we know that we will be coming back to benefit or not from what we did previously.

Reincarnation puts everything on a new perspective: No ego, no me, no others, not even recognition, but only and just pure love. Now, effectiveness equals no recognition, but who wants to be recognized if you get nothing in return? That's why few people truly change the world. The vast majority isn't interested in changing the world but focused on recognition. And that's why they are not very effective. If you wish to be effective, you need to forget yourself — your ego, your identity, and most importantly, your need for validation. And because most humans can't do this, they're just passing by, but not really leaving any significant change behind them.

About the Publisher

This book was published by the 22 Lions Bookstore.
For more books like this visit www.22Lions.com.
Join us on social media at:
Fb.com/22Lions;
Twitter.com/22lionsbookshop;
Instagram.com/22lionsbookshop;
Pinterest.com/22LionsBookshop.

www.ingramcontent.com/pod-product-compliance
Lightning Source LLC
Chambersburg PA
CBHW050450010526
44118CB00013B/1759